Passion, Pain & I

Immy Howarth

BookLeaf Publishing

India | USA | UK

Presentation by *BookLeaf Publishing*

Web: www.bookleafpub.com

E-mail: info@bookleafpub.com

ISBN: 9789357446082

First edition 2022

DEDICATION

For the family I have and the family I have chosen.

For all those who bring me joy. Thank you.

PREFACE

It has long been a goal of mine to share these words which are so personal to me, curated in moments of madness, pain, grief, ecstasy, joy and general emotional chaos. I was not sure on the theme of this collection until I had gathered half of its contents and realised that I have always used poetry to delve inside my mind.

These poems are the words of a child, the words of an adult, a student, a patient, an artist and, most importantly, the words of someone who is lost; writing to find themselves again.

Some of these poems have been written on train long journeys to see loved ones, some of them have been written at 3am in a state of drunken paralysis; but all of these poems have aided the clearing of my mind when it is too chaotic to understand what it is that I am feeling.

I have suffered with a chronic illness for most of my life. With this, physically I face challenges every day, never knowing if it will be a good or bad day until the moment I wake up.

This has taught me to listen to my body and mind, be resilient, brave and vulnerable and to know when to ask for help.It has been important in cementing together the building blocks of my identity.

I have always believed that my struggles are no more or less than anyone else's, that what makes us human is to be empathetic to the pains of others, and to listen not compare.

Pain is passion's alter ego. As with timber, allow the pain to dry and become something no longer alive, then burn it as fuel for passion. The world will be better and brighter for it.

Ink to paper, mind to mouth, these are the corners of my mind.

I can understand myself in writing; my struggles, my fears and my dreams. I hope you find something in this book that brings you peace, brings you joy and; and most importantly, helps you find yourself.

Open.

Ink stained final words
For truth to be understood
This... has to be good.

Fickle Bones

My heart is not fickle,
For she lives in fickle bones.

This heart is iron clad,
She pities the one that groans.

My shell is cracked and weak,
I have lived a thousand pains.

Each soul bonded to mine,
Brings light to tropical rains.

My fire is still burning,
Will burn forever in sight.

Have not they compassion,
Each soul has a fateful plight.

My sometimes agony,
To climb mountains in this storm.

The sun has burnt the night,
Time will take my final form.

My wishes to your friend,
I dream of showing you how.

Every night has to end,
We can jump in puddles now.

My apology here,
I mean it with compassion.

I see the pain I cause,
And do not think it fashion.

My stubborn pride is grave,
I should be given black coal.

My heart is not fickle,
For you save my aching soul.

Creation

Mother Courage Cuts deep,
Cautious blood doth seep.

Red-raw Compression down,
Curdling, semi-laughter, Clown.

Pirate Captain swaying blues,
Congregation softly Choose.

Compassion's loves great feat,
Friendless, star sign, obsolete.

These, are my Haunting Moons.

My Oasis

I'm stuck on No Man's Land
Floating on the seven seas
I feel the Kraken beneath me
Pulling my weakened knees

I'm stuck in Desert Dunes
Trekking across molten sands
I see the horizon close by
Too far to hold with hands

I'm stuck in outer space
Flying through Stardust City
Gravity does not hurt my bones
The moon feels no pity

Tender King

Hold me closer, tender thing,
Hold me tighter, golden King.
Envelope every inch of me,
Trace the steps, find the key.

Gobble me up, greedy beast,
Fill me up, a Titan's feast.
Feed me full on the cherry seeds,
Wet the roots of my needs.

Trace the steps, each finger leaves,
Trace the pains, my pleasure heaves.

Cry Baby

I don't want to cry
Because I miss you

I'd rather cry
Because you hurt me

Because if I cry
Because I miss you

It means
You have my heart.

Admittance

Icarus flew too close to the sun
Leviathan drowned in bitter seas

Odysseus wronged his righteous self
Vesper poisoned the honey bees

Ekaterin saw bloodthirsty men
Ymma sold her soul to the King

Oedipus kicked the vipers nest
Ulysses only horror did bring

Little Girl

Does anybody see the little girl?
She hides by day and night
In the closet where her mother said
She's forgotten how to fight

Can anybody hear the little girl?
She screams in muffled voices
Children are to be seen not heard
She shouts and has no choices

Has anybody found the little girl?
There's so many little girls gone
With fire burning in their hands and hearts
She is the little black swan

Does anybody see the little girl?
She's stood in the middle of the room
Proudly stood and smiling there
Her frozen mind is her tomb

Wilting Rose

Oh, my heart, like a wilting rose
As any other soul should see
Is denied the water of love
And I am in love with thee

Oh, my heart, like a wilting rose
What was once warm is now cold
Has seen a many summers pass
As the golden sun grows old

Oh, my heart, like a wilting rose
Shall be cursed with these blessed thorns
Will grow and make thy wounds of love
As my rose so dearly mourns

Oh, my heart, like a wilting rose
Will crumble at a touch of frost
The petals unfold before these
Gold petals sold at a cost

Oh, my heart, like a wilting rose
Shall see thy true spirit at last
When the shell of my broken rose
Will lay among others fast

Pompeii

I am a romantic,
Hopelessly too inclined
Dissolved in broken cynicism.

I feel so viciously,
Deeply non-affected at all
But broken by every atom.

Fates tectonic plates,
Splintering the numb ice
Of my ferocious love…

Afraid of ferocious fire,
Burning melted seascapes
Lying dormant for millennia.

It's better to feel pain,
Than that which leaves no feeling
But love is purest pain.

I cannot share my love,
For the Cork will surely pop
And Pompeii will not forgive me…

An exaggerated swarm,
Of three flowers into a thousand thorns
The bees are not friendly here.

I hate the love she feels,
Noah's overwhelming flood,
The Damned final blow.

Fed Up

I'm fed up of falling down
I'm fed up of reaching not quite far enough
I'm fed up of giving up
And I'm fed up of trying too hard.

I'm being choked by the same air
Through which I freefall
Unable to change course
My limbs are taken and my mind is trapped;
Like an emotional quadriplegic
I am poisoned by fear and hope

Conflicting tenses in my life,
Past is bad and present is bad;
Present is good and past is good.
But mostly the future is unknown
Looming, waiting and laughing

The future is gleaming and smiling
But it's pearly white teeth are sharp
The ancient MacHeath come to haunt me once
more

I Felt Pretty

I felt pretty tonight
I felt my confidence exude my every pore
With nothing but my own melancholy
My body moved to rhythms anew

I felt good tonight
But a lack of words thereafter
Reduced my confidence to guilt
I felt guilt tonight
For forcing a feeling I hoped falsely for

I felt stupid tonight
As you felt two pairs of hips
Neither which were mine
So swayed and ready for your attention

My body curved and moved
Each beat echoed in my bones
I thought you'd like me tonight
And if that should be so, it makes little sense to
me

I choose myself tonight
I feel the flesh on my bones

I feel the fire in my soul
I am the dancing devil tonight

Hades

Down in the fires of Hell,
Where iron melts to hellish gold,
A man sits on his skeleton throne
From, tales of Old.

His scarred face a reflection,
Of all his sins and more.
His slaves grovel before him,
Burning on the coal floor.

His brothers they did deceive him,
They took away his life,
And so he looks for revenge
To find a Hades Wife.

Be Safe, Be Sound

I want an evening
Wearing my troubles
Not on my sleeves;
But as feathers on my wings

I want to feel secure
Delve into the folds of me
And you, we lie together
Lie together, lay together

I want an evening
Holding my dreams tight
Not floating in ecstasy
But caught in safety

I want to feel sound
Each vibration, a bar put down
Stone cold and flat iron
And keeping me happily in

I want an evening
Where I am no prisoner
To the fear of passion
Instead I bathe in flowers

I want to feel a fire
So deep and fuelled by you
To quench this yearning
To be safe, to be sound

This Body

There is fat on this body
Beautiful curving fat that shapes my silhouette.
Soft and plush like nature's silky velvet
I feel warmth and comfort

My thighs shake and move,
Stagnant bodies exist only in false sisterhood
I grab my stomach, it's warmth heats my frozen hands
It is cold outside - this wind will howl and peel the skin off your face

I look in the mirror and see nothing but my smile
My naked body so intrinsically designed
A carving into the historic work of Mother Nature
Thoughts of body are placed too much on the body itself

My mind wishes to see nothing else
I cannot wish for what is not mine
I see Heaven when I see thee

There is fat on this body
And it is mine and I cherish it

Last Battlefield

It's awful lonely out here
Sitting on the side lines
Waiting for things that seem so near
I could wait a thousand times

I'm used to being forgotten
But not by those who love me
Child, do not be downtrodden
Like the sailor searching the lost sea

I do not like these words
I do not enjoy what they say
They say life is split in thirds
I don't want to work, sleep and play

I seem to have lost the feeling
The keys don't clatter as I tap them
My own sick ideas leave me reeling
Like a dragon in a dark, dark den

It's awful lonely out here
But no one understands me
Unresolved by a summer-garden beer
Nor with salty tears for spilt tea

I wish I could be the King,
The one with the gold hand.
Now it is he they praise and sing;
Loved by all in the Land

I think that any soul will do
I need someone to hold me tight
Not the drug you need to survive
But the one that keeps you high

There's a special place for me
I'm not afraid of myself
But I need, oh I need someone
To take the reins for a while

I See Through You

I can tell you the colour of your ex-lovers eyes
I can tell you the humour he would always
reprise
The world through his eyes is cruel and
unfounded
And yet you sit here, completely grounded

Echoing words I see, floating on cigarette smoke
You laugh and assume I am in on this joke
But the world is cruel and unfounded
And I feel anything but completely grounded

I can tell you what he whispered in your
forgotten memory
I can recall every detail from this fortnight
century
'Less than four hour' love takes hold of your
heart
Before the chequered flag flies before the engine
start

Is there something unrecognisable in the smile
on my lips?

Is there something inconceivable in the curve of
my hips?
Darkness becomes me in flattering light
Always a supporting actor to the star of the night

Is there power in the strength of my hand shake?
Is there a fear you feel, like it is you, who might
break?
Overwhelmingly, independently alone
A creeping desperation in my sultry tone

Is there a fire in the eyes of the woman over
there?
Is there a comedic glare in the heated wave of
my hair?
Neglecting Charming notions with spoiled spilt
tea
But you won't notice, go with her and forget me

Him

I lay in bed at night
And feel his body around me
Engulfing me
Seeping into my skin
Bleeding into being
Becoming one with me

I do not know this man
Yet have memorised every curve
Protecting me
Freeing my soul of pain
Taking my soul far away
Beckoning me to stay

I feel inside his heart
But have reached deeper than his gut
Exploring me
Begging to be taken
Fighting to be broken
Panicking me to live

I hear his steady breath
Though there is no body to breathe
Adoring me
Stroking each part of me

Touching each part inside
Commanding me to scream

I see nobody here
For pleasure is empty alone
Teasing me
Laughing because it can
Hiding because I want
Extracting him from me

Rainbow

There comes a time in all of our lives,
When sadness strikes.
But our mother's they sit us down-
And they say
"Don't you worry my child,

Because life is like this,
It will throw you away.
But just remember,
All that I have to say.

There's always a rainbow
Through the thickest storm,
And there's always a dream
Worth fighting for,

So sit with me and believe,
And open your heart,
The world my dear
Is a work of art."

But it's just a rhyme
From my childhood
That I can't forget
And I wonder if she would be proud

Of the cynic I've become

Because life is like this,
It has thrown me away,
So just remember
All that I have to say.

The rainbow will fade
If you give into the storm.
And the dreams we all dream
Kill us before we're born.

So how can I believe
Without my heart
The world, my dear,
Is falling apart.

But I promise you
The agony
Will soon fade away
Your mother was right and these are the words
That, she would say

"There's always a rainbow
Through the thickest storm,
So you have to hold on
To the cards that you have drawn,

So dance in the rain

And feel with your heart,
It's you, my dear,
Who is the work of art,"

Save Your Own Soul

It's stagnant green behind a metal grate,
The recognition plays itself around your finger
tip.
Flowing slowly, seeping gently out into your
footsteps and motions;
Hoping it's harsh structure will keep you safe.

Inanimate games and inconclusive fames,
Those same circles are run by creatures; around
and around.
Complaints about a world that can not be saved
by one,
Cannot be saved by one.

It's like a sinking ship buried into my gut,
The same horror a seaman faces against this
tsunami of guilt.
By why? My guilt is anger and my anger is love;
Built up to save and protect but not myself;
those walls they keep me in.

Too obvious, too glaring. Words can play tricks,

Focusing too hard on double meaning,
We forget the true embellishment of this world;
listen to what I say.
Serving each other in order to serve our need to
forget and idolise ourselves.

These words do not flow; they jar,
And struggle against the timelessness of life and
it's quirks;
Hoping, one day, to be understood and
recognised.
This gut wrenching feeling; the guilt that burns
our fire does nothing but toast marshmallows.

It's faith I have in myself which leads me to
doubt my word,
A fear so profound, no word can express its
danger.
It's darkness; falling and falling but not moving
as I wait so patiently;
For you, the world will stop for you - except it
won't.

It can't.

Around and around, the soullessness and
mundanity of truth;
It burns so deep in me that I scarcely feel my
soul.

A frozen beat, drumming away like a hollow
bone;
Feeling, fading, laughing and numbness all
envelope me at once.

This life where colour means black and white,
and black and white means colour,
This singular memory where happy things go to
die and rot;
These things have always been happy, will
easily tarnish, fade into abyss.
Everything has gone, no influence remains in the
memoirs of my memories.

I try to remember; who I am, who the world is.
I sit and shake and burn and freeze my mind and
thoughts within an inch of my own
understanding.
Of my own life.

I can't.

There's this hollow notion where she mentioned
she had been.
I feel it now, as I lay in the dark; fumbling and
mumbling to the Sand Man.
My arms are numb and weak, my mind is my
thriving companion;

He cannot remember why he fights, except that
he does - a Knights errant.

There is no hopelessness here,
There is beauty and life; surging and thriving;
hiding amongst the hidden things.
Only I can see beyond the blankness of my own
mind,
Observe and nurture the core of ice and fire that
burns so in myself.

You can't.

I see the shadowed figure; bending and cawing
and broken,
It calls to me and it's misery takes me captive;
the same ice thaws
It's way back, the figure is curiosity and naivety.
I am not, the frozen water begins my numbness
once more; these frozen chemicals are not the
same amongst minds.

I retract and more is seen as less, beauty faded
into brilliance;
Always another fight to look forward to and kiss
to regret.
Horror and honour both take place; next to
courage and confidence.

These things they walk hand in hand but the
puzzle pieces fit only my mind.

I cannot help you.

Close.

The best I can do
With my hands, and with my heart
So, forgive me, love.

www.ingramcontent.com/pod-product-compliance
Lightning Source LLC
LaVergne TN
LVHW010922200726
843509LV00013B/2036